A *Personal* PERSPECTIVE

A *Personal* PERSPECTIVE
FROM MY HEART TO YOURS

SONYA LANG HACKETT

TATE PUBLISHING & *Enterprises*

Published by Tate Publishing & Enterprises, LLC
127 E. Trade Center Terrace | Mustang, Oklahoma 73064 USA
1.888.361.9473 | www.tatepublishing.com

Tate Publishing is committed to excellence in the publishing industry. The company reflects the philosophy established by the founders, based on Psalm 68:11,
"The Lord gave the word and great was the company of those who published it."

Book design copyright © 2010 by Tate Publishing, LLC. All rights reserved.
Cover design by Stefanie Rooney
Interior design by Jeff Fisher

Published in the United States of America

ISBN: 978-1-61663-528-2
1. Religion, Christian Life, Devotional
2. Religion, Christian Life, Inspirational
10.06.28

Dedication

To my parents,
James Richard Lang and Christine Lang:

Dad: you were a tough and hardworking man. You never really expressed yourself a lot, but I always knew you loved me and were very proud of me for even my smallest accomplishments.

Mom: we shared a strong and special bond that even death cannot weaken. You truly loved me unconditionally; you disciplined me when necessary and taught me right from wrong through love. You are now my silent inspiration, and although you are no longer here to be able to witness and read my books, I feel your presence in the most divine way that is simply breathtaking. You were more than a fighter; you were a true warrior who devoted your entire life to giving and being the best you knew how to be to everyone. You never met a stranger and never shied away from sharing your personal experiences about the goodness of God. Throughout your struggles, heartaches, sorrows, and joy, I have become more than a conqueror, through Jesus. Thank you for encouraging me to get to know God for myself and for sharing your heart, words, whispers, tears, laughter, and thoughts.

Acknowledgments

First and foremost, thank you, God, for guiding me and helping me to write *A Personal Perspective*. It is through you that I find those humble beginnings in all of my work and everything I do. Since yielding to you and allowing you into my life, I have found true inspiration and contentment to share some of my personal testimonies, something I would have never done.

Julian Hackett: When I gave my heart to you, expression and creativity became my second nature. Through loving you, observing you, and listening to you, over the years I have learned how to truly embrace freedom, to always take risks, and never be afraid to try something new.

Hannah Christine Hackett, the joy of my life: I am honored to be your mother—what a joy and challenge wrapped into one. You have a distinct way about you that allows me to discover and see beyond what is directly in front of me. Your wild, unlimited, and creative mind has helped me to discover and hear unspoken words and draw and create art without art supplies or using my hands. You always give me something to write about and having you in my life is a priceless treasure.

Elestine Norman: You helped me to write my first book. I could not have done this without your commitment to both my blogs, and *A Personal Perspective*. Whenever I receive an edited blog back from you, I always see and feel your graceful smile even though you are miles away.

Tamika Nicole Johnson: Thank you for your dedication, continued support, creativity, and willingness to create layouts for my blogs. You are my inspiration!

When I decided I wanted to take a chance at publishing some of my blogs, I found out that publishing does cost, which did not deter me from pursuing and accomplishing my goal. Thanks to all of you who gave monetary gifts unreservedly and for your support. It means so much to me, and I am forever grateful.

Cortezria (Nicky) Harris: Before I developed enough courage to share some of my personal testimonies of faith with others, you encouraged me to share my life with the world through publication-even after I told you, "No way!" I appreciate your continued support and encouragement.

To all those who have taken the time to read my blogs: Thank you! Your feedback also inspired me to keep writing and was my confirmation to turn *A Personal Perspective* into a book so it can reach others near and far.

My sisters and brothers: In your own ways, you all helped to shape me, although we do not talk or see each other as often now that we are all adults. I've heard a lesson learned is best learned from experience, but being one of the youngest in the family provided me the sneak preview of what to do and what not to do, what works and what does not work by sitting back and observing. I guess being one of the youngest has its advantages.

J.R.: Thank you for introducing me to *my* tiger. Her heart is courageous and full of love — man does she love the wilderness — her senses are out of this world!

A special thank you to my closest friends: You are a special part of my family. Thank you for your words of encouragement.

Table of Contents

Introduction

Diligently seeking God, an optimistic perspective, clear vision, and hard work can take you to the mountaintop. Writing *A Personal Perspective: From My Heart to Yours,* was a huge leap of faith for me. It caused me to step back and truly let go, trusting God, and it became my deliverance.

As time passed, there has truly been some shedding of layers, allowing me to discover and tap into God's power through my personal relationship with him. The more I shared my testimonies of faith, the more I realized just how important it is for me to step aside and allow God to use me as his vessel and voice of inspiration, love, and hope. It is now over twenty-five years since the vision was given to me as a child, through Jesus, that I am introducing *A Personal Perspective*. It is not of my own heart that this publication was conceived, but through him, my hope and the one whom I humbly give my heart.

It is my sincere prayer that sharing some of my life's stories will change someone's life for the better. My greatest hope is that as you read the pages within this book from cover to cover, you will hear the hidden messages from God and that you will also desire to develop your own personal relationship with him. If you already have a personal relationship with him, I pray that it will be strengthened.

My Love Affair

We started out as friends, but over the years our relationship developed into a love affair like none I've ever heard of or read about because we never had physical contact. I had known J for a long time, and had been pretty good friends since middle school. As years passed, we spoke on occasion, but in most cases only when I needed something—how selfish of me. I would give him a call and, like clockwork, he was always there, readily available to listen.

Years passed and I went off to college. Before long I had met someone, Julian, whom six years later became my husband. Since I spent nearly all of my time with Julian while we dated, my friendship with

J faded somewhat, but never completely. I continued the relationship with J even as Julian and I became seriously involved.

Ironically, after Julian and I married, my relationship with J grew stronger. The first two years of our marriage was great, but a little rough at times. A month after our wedding, my mother passed suddenly. She and I were so close—I knew she loved me unconditionally, and her love was angelic. The love she demonstrated towards me was true, sincere, and graceful; it was felt in her smile, her touch, and from miles away. After her passing, my heart shattered into hundreds of tiny pieces. I knew she was better off in her passing, gone to be with the Lord, but I didn't know how to mend my broken heart. I carried on as if I was okay, but deep down inside I was hurting. I wore an invisible mask to hide my true feelings of grieving. I had always been known to be "strong" in coping with adversity—wearing the mask assisted in my task of faking my true emotions. Julian worked third shift at one of the local hospitals where he monitored and assisted patients and I dreaded the nights he had to work, during that time, while I mourned the loss of my mother.

While still trying to cope with my mother's death, and with adjusting to being alone during the nights—Julian's work schedule changed again. All within the same time frame, he started a new business in construction. Although I was excited for him and assisted him with the new business, I also knew it meant his having to be away from home more often. I felt more single than married at times. His busy schedule became a way for my lover and me to form a more intimate relationship. At that point in my life I needed more than conversation, I wanted him to hold and comfort me. It turned out that even asking that of him, he was readily available. This was the point of my relationship with J when we began to form a closer bond.

As much as I loved Julian, J and I shared a different type of bond and closeness. I knew Julian loved me and was proud to be my husband. When his schedule permitted, we had a blast together — he always knew how to make me laugh and captivate my mind. I thoroughly enjoyed the times I had him to myself. I also enjoyed our occasional weekend trips with our friends and family. Overall, Julian's time spent away with work and other things outweighed his time at home. This was the huge difference between he and J — availability. However, when Julian and I did spend time together, we were inseparable and any stranger could see that.

The more J and I talked, the closer I felt to him. He was so addictive because he always bandaged my

Sonya Lang Hackett

wounds to perfection; sometimes it happened immediately and other times it took a little longer. He even knew how to calm my fears.

While trying to cope with my mother's death, I found myself taking pain pills that were prescribed for me from previous procedures. I had held on to them, just in case I needed them. Some were from Julian's previous knee injuries and surgeries and now that I think about it, they were probably outdated. We both had a pretty high tolerance for pain so we never finished our prescriptions. Every single day, sometimes during the day, and always prior to bedtime, I'd take some sort of pain pill or sleeping pill. The pills eased me and became my sleep therapy. I'd started only taking them when Julian had to work at night because I could not sleep, but it quickly turned into a daily habit.

During the daytime or while I was amongst friends and family, no one felt or recognized my anguish and they even commended me for the strength I displayed while coping with my mother's death. On the other hand, Julian became very concerned when he'd ask for something to take for an occasional headache, but find there was never any medicine around the house. I had taken all of his prescription medicines, what was left of them, without his permission or knowledge. When I told him

18

what I had done, he cleared the house of pain pills and medicines. If I needed them for real pain, I had to go through him. That is when I discovered I had a serious problem; I was addicted.

I recall my first night trying to sleep without any pain medicine or sleeping pills after Julian hid or discarded them. He was at work and I could not sleep. I drove myself to tears that night, not because I was hurting, but because I did not have anything to take. After exhausting myself searching for pills, I laid down and tried to fall asleep. I wanted the pills because I knew they would help me fall asleep. I was so tired and wanted someone to talk to; I then remembered I could call J. Like always, he was able to talk and the first thing he said to me was, "You don't need the pills, Sonya." Those words released healing to my soul, and that was the last night I had a burning desire to take pain pills for anything other than real physical pain. I have to be seriously ill or in intolerable pain in order to put a prescription pain pill into my mouth. I was delivered that night.

It was about six months after our wedding day and after trying to get pregnant, I was finally with child. My father passed shortly after we got the news we were pregnant. It was an exciting time for us, a time when I had to push with all of my might to move past losing my parents and switch into another gear — motherhood. My dad suffered a serious illness and had been in and out of the hospital prior to his death, so I was able to brace myself a little better in accepting the loss, plus I had a much closer relationship with my mom. I was also able to move on more peaceably because I knew how much suffering he had endured.

After my father's passing and getting pregnant, I figured out a way to keep busy, and the thought of calling J wasn't just a thought anymore — it was something I looked forward to and depended upon. He had grown to be my confidant and best friend. I yearned to talk with him daily. The closeness J and I shared took my mind away from other things — I didn't complain about Julian's busy schedule as often or hardly ever. My feelings of loneliness transformed into contentment because J was always there. Julian even appreciated the change.

Having J in my life became my lifeline; with his help and love, I grew stronger every day. I had moved past grieving and felt happier, especially since Julian and I were about to become parents. Whenever I did experience periods of loneliness or was upset with Julian, J would even soften my heart to forgive Julian and reminded me to walk in love. He took care of me and gave me strength I never knew I possessed, especially during some of my darkest and weakest moments.

Many of my family members often wondered and even asked how I remained so content while Julian had to be away with work or his bowling. Prior to becoming pregnant, I traveled with him on most of his bowling trips. However, I was still asked by some, "How do you do it?" I've even had some say to me directly, "The only way you can be that content and happy is if you have your own extracurricular activities." My answer to all the questions and speculations is this; "I have been having an affair for a long, long time. This affair has become everything to me and has been the source of my strength, peace, and happiness. I proudly introduce him, my Lord and personal Savior, Jesus Christ. The one who held me and consoled me during long sleepless nights, the one who whispered comforting words into my spirit and guided me, and the one who mended my broken heart and gave me courage to fight when I had no strength of my own. Had it not been for my pursuing him, I could still be addicted to pills or could have given up a long time ago. I am still standing and enjoying my life only because of his love, grace, and mercy."

I have had a spiritual love affair with my Lord for as long as I can remember, and our relationship continues to grow the more I seek him. My happiness cannot be defined by anything or anyone, for my true freedom has come through him. I can honestly say that in all of my life, he has never misguided nor forsaken me. He has been my comfort during every season — good and bad. I turn to him and rely on him with all of my strength and in him I am made whole. Through him, I am also able to continue pressing my way, walking in love, and walking in obedience when I want to do things my way — walking by faith when all my circumstances tell me it's over.

One thing I have learned about my spiritual love affair with my Lord and my marriage is that, if we share the relationship with our Lord and grow together as one, nothing — not even imbalance or heartache can destroy the bond. If the Lord is not the center of the relationship, the bond of marriage is at risk, subject to fall apart and will not sustain trials. We must consciously choose our Lord, and he must remain first and foremost — the center of our marriage and lives. If we exclude him and become self-driven or self-reliant, then at some point that which we consider a success will eventually fail.

My affair with Jesus has been the thread that held Julian and I together through many years of trials. Many times when I felt like quitting or became frustrated, I would stop Julian and ask him to pray with me, regardless of how busy his schedule was at the time. There were many times I would call him mid-day and ask him to stop what he was doing for a minute so we could pray together. Before he could rest after a long day's work or prior to him going back to work, I'd lay with him and pray with him — sometimes while he slept. The affair I had with my Lord was the force that strengthened me in those weaker moments of our marriage.

> "Wherefore they are no more twain, but one flesh."
>
> (Matthew 19:6, KJV)

A Mustard Seed of Faith

Think about the size of a mountain; now think about the size of a mustard seed, which measures around one millimeter in size. Is that the measure of faith Jesus requires us to have for the impossible to become possible? I used to think I had to have great faith in order for miracles to happen in my life. However, what I have learned is that if we plant that tiny seed of faith and nurture it, giving it water and proper sunlight, it will produce a healthy harvest. Likewise, if we continue to walk diligently seeking God by studying his holy word and praying, our tiny seeds of faith will grow and what we thought was impossible for us would become our reality.

Our daughter, Hannah, will occasionally from time to time take some of the dry beans from our kitchen pantry and plant them all around the house. On one particular afternoon, I had come home from work and was standing at my kitchen sink doing the dishes. While looking out the window and observing birds in the backyard, I stood there thanking God for his wonderful creations. At that time, I had been studying faith and was on a twenty-one day fast. My focus shifted from the birds to the single bean Hannah had set on the windowsill in a Ziploc bag; she placed a wet paper towel inside it to give it moisture. To my surprise, that bean had grown into a tiny little stalk with several small roots protruding around the bottom of the Ziploc bag. I noticed the top of the bean had sprouted. Still standing at the sink, I turned and noticed she had another bean plant growing in a plastic cereal container that had grown much stronger and taller. As I observed it more closely, I noticed one of the leaves had begun to turn black, so I called her into the kitchen to see if she wanted me to throw it out.

"Hannah!" I shouted from the kitchen. I heard her little feet running towards the kitchen before she entered. "Yes, mom," Hannah replied, standing attentively, gazing into my eyes and waiting for me to continue. "Baby, I think your plant is dying, do you want me to throw it out?" She took it out of my hands and observed it carefully and cheerfully. "Oh no, Mom, it's okay!" She turned on the faucet just enough for a steady drip and held the bean plant under the stream to water it; then she ran back to what she was doing as carefree as a wild buck in an open forest. After she left the kitchen, I stopped what I was doing to carefully observe the bean plants.

A few days passed and to my surprise, the leaf that had turned black had fallen off and more new leaves had replaced it. Not only were there new leaves, the plant had doubled in height. God began to minister to my heart; "That's just how faith works." We start with a little seed of belief and from that tiny seed we reap enormous growth.

At one point whenever my husband or I would walk outside or prepare to mow our lawn, we would see all types of little plants growing up from out of the ground where Hannah had taken fists full of beans and seeds and threw them all over the yard. She didn't even turn back the soil, but happily and without a worry, tossed them with expectation that all of them would grow — and they did; it was amazing!

Whenever I saw her checking on her plants, giving them water or turning the dirt, I was reminded of how we are to walk by faith and not by sight. When we plant seeds, we plant them anticipating and hopeful that whatever we plant will eventually grow. Even though they start out as tiny as a seed, we believe and wait eagerly and patiently for that seed to transform into a plant or flower. Just as Hannah took the time to give care to her plants, we must give the same care to our faith walk.

Start today by planting that seed of faith. Regardless of what circumstances you may be facing—illness, loss of a loved one, child on drugs, violence, loss of a job—regardless of how big your mountain may be, know that nothing is too hard for God. He will see you through as you trust in him. When we continue in prayer and studying the word of God, we water and nurture those seeds that pertain to the situation. Before you realize it, the focus shifts from the problem to magnifying God and that which you thought was impossible becomes possible for you. Although some seeds may take longer to produce fruit, once that seed is planted, it will bring forth rewards.

"And when they were come to the multitude, there came to him a certain man, kneeling down to him, and saying, Lord, have mercy on my son: for he is lunatic, and sore vexed: for ofttimes he falleth into the fire, and oft into the water. And I brought him to thy disciples, and they could not cure him. Then Jesus answered and said, O faithless and perverse generation, how long shall

I be with you? How long shall I suffer you? Bring him hither to me. And Jesus rebuked the devil; and he departed out of him: and the child was cured from that very hour. Then came the disciples to Jesus apart, and said, why could not we cast him out? And Jesus said unto them, Because of your unbelief: for verily I say unto you, If ye have faith as a grain of mustard seed, ye shall say unto this mountain, Remove hence to yonder place; and it shall remove; and nothing shall be impossible unto you."

(Matthew 17:14-20, KJV)

I'll Wait for You, Oh Lord

The waiting season can be a brutal process simply because as human beings we want everything *right now*. Not only do we want everything right now, we want everything the way we want it. What I have found during some of my waiting seasons is that when I am waiting on God for an answer or for a specific blessing, I sometimes become frustrated, impatient, and out of order.

Why do we get so bent out of shape sometimes when it seems that everything is going wrong? After all, God did say he was a present help in the time of trouble. Not only that, but he encourages us: "But they that wait upon the LORD shall renew their strength; they shall mount up with wings as eagles; they shall run, and not be weary; and they shall walk, and not faint" (Isaiah 40:31, KJV).

Four things that occur when we become impatient:

1. We sometimes get off course from God's plan for our lives, which may cause setbacks and take years to correct.

2. We *allow* the enemy victory over us; and his plan is to kill, steal, and destroy God's children.

3. We completely miss out or, as I jokingly say sometimes, "miss the boat" (referring to those who did not board Noah's Ark) on the very thing for which we've prayed and longed.

4. We stop trusting God, which over time separates us from him.

When we become impatient, we step out of his will. Although you may accept the temporary gratifications that inevitably shift you from God's plan, you run a greater risk of loss and failure. One thing I stress to others and what I find essential to understand is that God's will for you may totally go against the very thing you desire. This is how we sometimes miss the boat and drown. I generally think about those individuals seeking a mate. I often hear people describe to perfection what they desire in a mate, from their height, size, color of eyes, what type of career they have, what type of car they drive, and even down to their skin complexion. It is okay to have a general idea of what you desire, but often-times the husband or wife God tailor-made just for you may not be exactly what you want or conform to your checklist. Unfortunately, you spend many years searching for Mr. or Miss Right when he or she is usually within arm's reach.

As I continue to seek God during my seasons of waiting and also during my seasons of harvest, my patience increases to the point of contentment. When I look back over my life I can clearly see how the hand of God not only kept me, but also truly parted seas, moved mountains, and turned one fish into a mighty feast. You see, when you learn to walk in confidence rather than worry, grief, frustration, resentment, or fear, all the biblical stories become relative to your situations no matter what season you are experiencing.

A while ago I made a decision that I struggled with, at first, for fear of losing someone. Since mak-ing that choice, I completely let go and allowed God to take full control over my life. Many did not understand how I could do what I did, and some even questioned whether my decision was truly made out of love. I am not only confident that I did the right thing, but I trusted God. My greatest desire is to live within God's will and to walk in love. By making that choice and sticking with it, I am learning to look at the bigger picture — God. Now, during my waiting season of transition and more decisions, I find myself saying, "I'll wait for You, Oh Lord and Lord I trust you."

"Trust in the Lord with all thine heart."

(Proverbs 3:5, KJV)

How to Wait Upon the Lord

Waiting can be a brutal process simply because it appears that nothing is happening or changing in your favor. Sometimes, it may even seem like God is nowhere to be found and has abandoned you. The very thing you are seeking God for seems so far from your reach, impossible and farther, and farther away from your reality. That is why we are to walk by faith and not by sight (2 Corinthians 5:7). Walking by faith should change your perception of the way things are. Instead of wondering if, when, or how long, you should begin to walk in expectation believing that no matter when the manifestation of your blessings takes place or when your deliverance occurs, it *will* happen. Therefore, you wait with expectancy, peace, joy, contentment, and an attitude of gratitude knowing that God will deliver as he promised.

How do you handle those moments when your circumstances come crashing down upon you like tidal waves beating upon a beachfront? Each thrust of turbulent water from the waves pushes the shoreline back farther washing away the sand, which represents your circumstances. Depending upon how strong the force of the wind and in which direction it is blowing, it causes the shoreline to erode and water from the ocean now begins to beat upon your house—you. How do you come out victorious in situations that nearly destroy your home; how do you protect yourself from destruction?

I have encountered some life storms that nearly destroyed my faith, such as the loss of my baby in miscarriage. During some of my waiting seasons, I felt as if the seasons of the year passed me as swiftly as day transitioned into night—I saw winter, spring, summer, and fall seemingly two and three times before my deliverance. Did I faint, worry, lose faith or quit? I must say that I did from time to time. I did those things the moment I took my eyes off God. Each time I placed my focus on my circumstances, they grew larger and more unbearable. However, the moment I switched my focus back on God, he became larger and my circumstances grew smaller. That is one of the ways I have remained, and continue to remain victorious; I began to pay attention to God.

How do you wait upon the Lord and remain victorious despite your odds? How do you walk in expectation rather than worry and fear? These twelve steps have proven true and are my support for surviving any season:

1. Walk by faith and not by sight (2 Corinthians 5:7). Read and meditate on the word of God by placing your focus on him rather than your circumstances.

2. Wait with expectation — know that God is with you and will see you through (Psalm 62:5). When you wait in expectation, you wait with a "knowing" with confidence that God will see you through your situation.

3. Wait with thanksgiving as if it is already done (Psalm 34:1). As you wait in expectation you also become delighted and thankful — praise God for what you believe he will do in your life.

4. Humble yourself and admit that you need God (James 4:10). It is hard to wait on God or anyone with an arrogant attitude. Some things are too much for us to handle on our own; humility opens the door for solutions and help—it is okay to ask for help and admit to him that you need him.

5. Diligently seek God (Hebrews 11:6). Don't just pray one day for your problems to be solved. Don't stop praying, don't stop believing, and don't stop reading God's holy word. When you diligently seek God, you strengthen your relationship with him.

6. "Submit yourselves therefore to God. Resist the devil, and he will flee from you." (James 4:7, KJV). Resist temptations of doing things your own way or taking the easy way out or giving into your flesh.

7. Make time for God (Hebrews 11:6). Prioritize your schedule and set aside 'alone time' specifically for you and God—reading his word, praying and meditating on God's scripture.

8. Speak positive things over your life (Proverbs 18:21). Avoid speaking negative things about your circumstances regardless how bad things may seem at the time; instead find something positive to say about your life and place your focus on positive things.

9. Avoid negative people. Guard your thought-life and heart. Do not involve yourself in gossip or allow others to overwhelm you with their complaining and ungratefulness. It really is okay to walk away or distance yourself (Proverbs 4:23).

10. Lean not to your own understanding but trust in the Lord at all times (Psalm 62:8, and Proverbs 3:5). When trusting God to work out your situation, trust that no matter how things work out, God knows what is best for you and will work your situation out to his glory.

11. Obey God when he speaks to you and be prepared to forget about yourself and your own desires (Matthew 4:4). Learn to pray for God's will to be done in your life rather than your own will. Trust that God's will is always best for your life.

12. Be prepared for the fight by putting on the whole armor of God and ready to "Endure the process" (Ephesians 6:11). Be still and know that God is who he says he is (Psalm 46:10). He is the Alpha and Omega, the beginning and the ending, which is, and which was, and which is to come, the Almighty (Revelation 1:8, KJV). He is our refuge and strength a very present help in trouble (Psalm 46:1, KJV). Prepare for battle by knowing what the word of God has to say about your situations. Understand how God sees you and how he works — study God's word daily.

Our wait tends to become long or seem long because we make it that way by losing faith. Each time we lose faith, we take a few steps backwards. We stumble and fall, quit, and get up again. Nevertheless, it is all a part of the process to make you stronger. The process is not meant for God to hurt nor torture you, but for him to prepare and strengthen you for what is to come and also for your testimony to help others. I used to hear my mother say, "I know what I know because I have been there and have seen God move on my behalf. I know only God could have brought me through." In order to truly know God and understand how he works without just reading about him, you are going to have to endure the process of waiting. Don't give up, and don't fret, for the Lord your God is not only with you but knows where you are headed. If you pay attention to him and obey him, he will lead you to your Promised Land. In the meantime, enjoy your life and trust God. He will deliver you in his time, when he knows you are ready.

How will you ever know what God has for you if you constantly take the easy way out by turning to instant satisfaction and gratification? How will you ever witness God's infinite power if you never stand tests of times? For once in your life, stop running and endure your seasons with an attitude of faith so that you can taste and see that the Lord is good—he *is* who he says he is.

> "My soul, wait thou only upon God; for my expectation is from him. He only is my rock and my salvation: he is my defense; I shall not be moved. In God is my salvation and my glory: the rock of my strength, and my refuge, is in God. Trust in him at all times; ye people, pour out your heart before him: God is a refuge for us. Selah."
>
> (Psalm 62:5—8, KJV)

Pain for a Purpose

I recall one night at the gym, I had begun my thirty-minute cardio session on the elliptical glide machine. After being on the equipment for nearly twenty-five minutes, I caught an extremely bad cramp in my right side. I always increase and decrease my resistance levels along with speed during intervals to get my best burn. However, just when I increased the resistance from level eight to ten, the pain from the cramp cut so sharply into my side that I couldn't take a deep breath. I was exhausted and hot but determined to finish; sweat ran down my scalp onto my face and on down to my neck into my shirt and from my arms to my hands. As I gripped the handles on the machine for support, my sweaty palms weakened my grip causing them to slide. I leaned my body into the handles for better support while I pushed the pedals. I was soaked in sweat from head to toe, and hoped I wasn't going to have to quit before my time expired.

I slowed down almost to a pause, the lights on the machine flashed the word *pause* in red letters, which meant if I did not increase my speed quickly, the machine would reset itself and erase the stats for my workout. I did my best not to stop and kept moving. Slowing down a little, this time almost to a complete stop, I fought hard to push past the sharp-cutting knot of pain in my side. At that point, I took a slow, and deep breath — oh, how it hurt! I closed my eyes tightly and slowly exhaled calmly with my eyes still closed. The pain was so intense that I almost stopped, but after pushing to inhale and exhale a few long, deep, and slow breaths, the pain began to subside and I found strength to keep my feet pedaling faster with a steadier momentum. With a sigh of relief, I drank a little water, turned the volume back up on my iPod and the rest was history. I finished like a champ, and surpassed my set time. One more session completed towards the whole purpose of my workout — to lose weight and become healthier.

As I pushed through my pain, the word *purpose* staggered in my mind. What is the purpose behind our actions or our commitments? I then thought about the purpose behind the suffering of Jesus — the shedding of his blood on the cross...the purpose God had when he literally gave his only begotten son. I am not in any way comparing the pain of my side cramp to the crucifixion of Jesus and although the comparison is very extreme, I want you to think about purpose. Examine the purpose and commitment — the goal of our Lord when he sacrificed his only son. His purpose was for our benefit so that we may have eternal life through his loving grace and mercy — forgiveness of our sins (John 3:16).

Although I was in excruciating pain (nothing in comparison to Jesus) trying to push my way through my workout, I knew I could not stop. My focus was on my purpose, why I needed to honor my commitment. I could have stopped to take a break, but I knew if I stopped, the probability of continuing my workout was slim to none. Was a break worth diverting from my purpose for being in the gym to begin with?

Our all-powerful God could have intervened during the trial of Jesus before the crucifixion. He could have diverted from his purpose and not allowed his son to endure such pain, but he didn't. As inhumanly, gruesome, and grim Jesus' suffering was, the purpose was greater. God's purpose was fulfilled through his son's suffering — forgiveness!

Sometimes we need to reflect back to our purpose for our commitments—why we do the things we do. Why do you give up? Why do you remain committed? Are you willing to endure pain for a purpose—for a greater reward? Pain can deter one from their commitments quicker than anything. I admit, anguish has caused me to divert at times from the course of my commitments. However, as I grow older and wiser, I realize that generations following mine may be affected by my actions or lack of actions. My daughter, Hannah, who watches everything I do—I owe it to her to remain committed to my purpose of becoming better in everything I do.

God's grace—think about the opportunity we gained through his sacrifice for our purpose to be set free through repentance from sin and bondage. In comparison, there is no greater example why we should not be able to endure pain for a purpose. I used this extreme example because many times we need *extreme* to keep us motivated and committed.

"For God so loved the world, that he gave his only begotten Son, that whosoever believeth in him should not perish, but have everlasting life."

(John 3:16, KJV)

For This Child I Prayed

Prior to becoming pregnant with our daughter Hannah, I had another loss—Julian. Both pregnancies were complicated. Upon turning sixteen weeks with Julian, I began to miscarry and had dilated a few centimeters by the time I arrived at my doctor's office. Since I was only sixteen weeks, I had no idea what to expect even though I had miscarried previously at about eight weeks. I was devastated, but trusted that my doctor knew what she was doing—she was wonderful and if anyone could calm my nerves, she could. Thankfully her practice was somehow connected to the hospital, so transporting me was an easy task. Easy, but the longest ride I'd known at the time.

Holding on to every ounce of faith I had, I grabbed for my husband's hand, tears streaming down my face. Everything was happening so fast and some things I cannot remember. I only remember the second day in the hospital listening to my doctor explain to us how I would have to deliver Julian, even though the likelihood for him to survive was slim to none; he was simply too underdeveloped. Although he was tiny, he was alive and his heartbeat remained strong during labor.

Finally, after laboring for hours, it was time to push. My doctor had coached me to safely delivering Julian. I took a deep sigh of relief, but wondered how he was doing. The nurse took him out of the room immediately. My doctor gave my husband and me a moment to ourselves and then re-entered the room to see if we wanted to see Julian since he was still alive; surprisingly, with a strong heartbeat. Reluctantly, I agreed to hold him in my arms and see his tiny, frag-ile, and underdeveloped body. He was wrapped in a small hand-woven blanket. As I looked down into his face at his closed eyes, and shiny, almost translucent skin, I felt so close to God — his tiny miracle of life. Julian was still alive at the time. I felt sad and proud all at the same time; proud that I had the opportunity to spend time with him, and sad that he wasn't going to survive. He stopped breathing about an hour after I saw him, only two days away from my twenty-third birthday on July 2, 1997. This experience taught me that some situations are created for the purpose of strengthening us for what's to come — strength to endure another complicated pregnancy.

After the loss of Julian, I knew I still wanted to have a child someday. Three years after losing Julian, my husband and I began making plans to try again. After we became pregnant with Hannah, my doctor became a very special part of our family. She was committed to helping us get through this pregnancy successfully.

I did not have a problem getting pregnant, but carrying a child seemed to be the hard part for me. I recall several mornings and many times throughout the day while pregnant, I would be praying softly to God to bless our baby. The unbelievable part about my pregnancy was that before I had an ultrasound to determine the sex of our baby, I already knew I was carrying a girl and her name was going to be Hannah. My husband, Julian, like he normally does, thought I was joking but I knew she was our little Hannah and I began talking to her and calling her by her name.

My water broke the day I turned twenty-four weeks into my pregnancy, and Hannah was born the third day of my twenty-seventh week. I spent one month in the hospital on bed rest. Our plans certainly do not always coincide with God's plan, that's for sure. Since he is all-powerful, I trusted that he would take care of both of us, even though she only weighed two pounds and fifteen ounces. At birth, she was very sick and was immediately placed on the ventilator. I wasn't able to see her until later that night. Although her body was small, lying there in the incubator hooked to all the machines and monitors, she was so beautiful and I couldn't even see her eyes. After I saw her, I had a sigh of relief that she made it.

Two days after her birth she was removed from the ventilator and was administered oxygen for about two weeks. I recall this day vividly because I was standing there looking at her tiny body inside the incubator. She was a lot smaller after coming off the machine. I noticed her tiny body was shaking and quivering. It bothered me to see her like that so I asked the nurse what was wrong with her. She told me Hannah's body was jittery because she was trying to adapt to her new surroundings—outside of my womb. At that moment, I felt as if I had failed her and began to cry to the point where I had to leave her bedside.

As I walked down the hospital hallway, I was fighting back my tears searching for the closest restroom so I could stop to pray. I leaned against the wall in the single bathroom and prayed for God's Holy Spirit to comfort Hannah and keep her in his perfect peace—at that point I gave her back to God and thanked him for blessing me to become her mother. I must have stayed in the bathroom for about fifteen minutes praying and talking with the Lord. That evening, instead of returning to the Neonatal Intensive Care Unit (NICU), I went home and trusted that God was going to honor my prayer to keep Hannah safe and healthy in his care.

The very next morning I headed to the hospital after some much needed rest. To my surprise, she was resting peacefully and calmly — no quivering or jitters at all! I remembered my prayer and smiled to myself thanking God for honoring my prayer request. She was in God's hands for sure.

Hannah grew stronger and stronger every day. The nurses always stated she was a good baby and that she hardly ever cried. Some even began to wonder if she could cry because she rarely ever made a fuss about anything — they didn't know about my talk with Jesus, so I told them she was just fine and I didn't have any concerns about her.

She remained in the hospital for fifty-one days until we were able to take her home. She weighed a little over five pounds. From that point on, she had some tough times with reactive airways disease, which was always a problem during the cold and flu season. For a while, we were certainly acquainted with the emergency room. Around four years of age she began to grow out of the disease and was cleared by the specialist to discontinue her year-round and seasonal breathing treatments.

Although I had previously experienced the loss of a child prior to Hannah's birth, I was unsure whether she would make it or not. I held on to my faith as I laid in the hospital thirty days praying with her and talking to her — my faith increased daily. God has truly blessed Hannah to be a normal little girl, full of life and joy — sometimes full of so many questions that I often do not have the answers, but she is our blessing and has changed my life in so many ways. As a result of her birth, I have a new level of respect for parents who have children with disabilities and serious illnesses; my heart goes out to them. Seeing your child sick takes a lot out of you, but also helps you to realize that there is indeed a higher power. My higher power is God — he has helped me along this journey of parenting and has kept us during all the trying times. There were days when we didn't have enough funds to purchase medicine or when we had to decide if we would purchase medicine for our sick daughter or go without — we went without a lot, but the sacrifice and the reward in return is priceless.

"For this child I prayed; and the LORD has given me my petition, which I asked of him."

(1 Samuel 1:27, KJV)

Don't Quit

It was the second semester of my freshman year at St. Augustine's College and time to validate and finalize my spring class schedule. After standing in line in the student union to sign up for my classes, I was told I had a red flag and needed to report to the financial aid office immediately. Pretty disheartening after such a long wait in line, I thought. Walking away feeling a little discouraged, I peddled my way through another long line at the financial aid office.

The line turned out not to be so bad, but I was eager to find out the nature of my 'red flag'. I pulled one of the assistants I knew to the side, "Can you *please* help me? I was sent here to clear a red flag on my account."

She pulled my file electronically and gave me the horrific news, "We can't register you because you were not awarded enough money to cover your tuition. I can set you up on a payment plan for the balance."

"What? I cannot afford to pay all of that! What are my options?" She responded, "Well, there are other options, but due to your grade point average you are not covered."

"But, is there anything else I can do? What about work study?"

"I am sorry, there are no other options at this time."

I was devastated. I headed straight for the pay phone to call my mother. "Ma, I have really bad news. I have to come back home." Tears of frustration and disappointment streamed down my red cheeks.

"I need you to come get me on Friday, I am not eligible for financial aid because of my grades."

"What?" My mom replied in a disappointing tone. "What do you mean?"

"Momma, can you come get me, I will explain it all later. Maybe there is something I can do between now and Friday."

I could not settle for quitting and going back home. Although I went back to my dorm room and started packing my belongings, my mind was going a hundred miles a minute thinking of possible solutions. I was not going to take no for an answer. After about an hour of gathering my things, my roommate, Tee, returned. "What are you doing?"

"I have to go back home; I don't have all the money I need to register for my classes and I can't do that until my account is settled." She was still in shock and started offering suggestions. I had forgotten that her assignment for work-study was in the Financial Aid Office. I pleaded, "You have to talk to her for me, and maybe there is something she can do to help." Whew, for a second, I saw a bit of sunshine peeking through my clouds. I later prepared to take a walk around the track to clear my mind. Our dorm mother was standing in the lobby and stopped me to ask what I had done over my winter break.

I confided in her about my situation and she flat out asked me, "Can you honestly tell me you have exhausted every possible venue for you to stay in school?" I told her that I was waiting to hear back from the Financial Aid Office.

She replied, "Don't quit until you do." The sun was shinning brighter and brighter.

"I will not quit."

Later that night Tee told me she had spoken with Mrs. Fields and that she wanted me to stop by her office the next morning. I never prayed so hard. Daylight finally broke and I eagerly jumped out of bed, got dressed, and headed to her office for my appointment. Anxiously waiting to speak with her, I sat on the edge of my seat, butterflies fluttering all around my stomach, and sweating palms. I experienced all the symptoms of a person who is a nervous wreck. Finally a voice called, "Ms. Lang, Mrs. Fields will see you now." Taking a deep breath, I stood to my feet and walked into her office and sat in a chair directly across from her desk. "How can I help you?" She had such a welcoming personality and smile. I scanned her desk and saw a little plaque that had a bible verse on it. That calmed my nerves a little and I felt a whole lot better, feeling God's presence through the scripture.

I cleared my throat and spoke softly. "Well, I do not have enough financial aid to continue through the full school year, and I cannot go back home." She reviewed my account and asked me if I knew I had received an incomplete for one of my mandatory classes.

"An incomplete … that can't be correct." I replied.

"Well, that is why we cannot award you financial assistance. In order for you to receive financial assistance, you must maintain a certain GPA and you are off by a few points. What I suggest is go and speak with the professor to see if you can work something out with him. If you can, come back to see me and I can help you."

After leaving Mrs. Field's office I did not stop until I reached Mr. Tyndall's office. I prayed all the way there, walking quickly, hoping he would be available. Sure enough, he was in his office. I confidently walked in; "Mr. Tyndall, do you have a minute?"

"Sure. What brings you here?"

"Well, I received an incomplete for your class last semester and I honestly do not think that it is correct."

"Well let's take a look." My heart was pounding as if I had jogged the entire campus in anticipation of hearing his verdict. "Well it looks like you did not show up for my final exam. I have you absent the day of my final."

I rebutted, "That is not correct; I took the final! Not only did I take the final, but I thought I did quite well on it." Since he had no record of my exam and I could not recall the test, we compromised and I would complete a research paper that would carry the same weight as my final exam. That was definitely music to my ears because writing any paper was like a trip to the candy store for me.

I completed the assignment, submitted it the following morning and hovered over Mr. Tyndall until he graded it so I could immediately report my grade back to Mrs. Fields. Not surprisingly, I received an A on the assignment. I returned to the Financial Aid office and waited for about ten minutes to speak with

Mrs. Fields. Tee walked up to report for work study and informed Mrs. Fields I had been waiting downstairs to see her.

I believe the cheer on my face was as bright and radiant as the California sun. I enthusiastically sat down across from her once again. "Well, I spoke with Mr. Tyndall and he changed my grade from the incomplete to a B. Would you believe he recorded my grade incorrectly?" Mrs. Fields returned the smile and immediately went to work finding available money so I could hurry and make the deadlines to register for my classes to stay in school. I was assigned work study to cover the balance on my account for the semester. Just as expected, I loved my job assignment and met three wonderful ladies who became my mentors and friends.

I could have easily given up when I was advised I could not receive financial aid, but what I learned from that experience is, you will never know what lies ahead or around the corner if you give up. For the first time in my life, I stood alone in prayer, determined not to quit. I relied on a scripture my mother had shared with me about being still and trusting God. Being still to me did not mean to stop trying, but to realize who was my helper. After replaying what had happened within three days after being told I either had to come up with a lot of money or go home, I saw the hand of God at work as I remained committed to stay in school. Although I had to speak with people, and ask for help, it was God's favor that allowed all the doors to open as I walked through them. Spiritually, I was being still — I trusted God would help me and He did. My parents did not have to pick me up at the end of that week, which was music to my mother's ears.

If you are at a crossroads and think there are no available options, please do not quit. Perseverance requires you to challenge yourself, take risks, ask questions, ask for help, set aside pride, and be patient. Was the fight to stay in school worth it? Going home was not an option.

"Be still, and know that I am God."

(Psalm 46:10, KJV)

"Look Momma, I'm Riding!"

I had been trying to teach Hannah how to ride her bike. It was a gift for her fifth birthday and was much bigger than she was, so we knew it would take some time to learn how to ride it all by herself. She had shown more interest than ever in wanting to ride her bike around the neighborhood. This journey had been a little disheartening, but mostly pure joy. Her days of frustration became a greater reward for each of us as she improved day by day; and, for me, the reward came as I thought about faith — it is by works that faith is made perfect. Works and faith must cohabitate in order for us to truly prosper and succeed at anything (James 2:14, 26, KJV). One can work and become very successful obtaining great wealth, but without God, it will profit him nothing (Matthew 16:26, KJV). I also thought about my relationship with Jesus, as his child, and how he watches over me as a parent.

One evening she surprised me while riding her bright pink bike. Thank God there is a long hallway, which allows enough space for her to practice on evenings that I have to seriously multi-task. It was unlike many times when I stood beside her holding the bike up so she could master the pedaling concept, yet grunting and stumbling all the way.

The open floor plan at the front of our house allows me to see into the living room and partially down the hallway while I am in the kitchen. This time she eagerly asked, "Ma, can you just stay in the kitchen and watch me when I come by?" She didn't want my help. I thought, "Man! What a nice change of pace."

With my back turned as I prepared a small meal for dinner, I saw movement from the corner of my eyes and even heard a few bumps and murmuring. As I turned quickly to see what Hannah was doing, I saw the most beautiful sight; she was upright on her bike. She had managed to balance herself for a short distance, but as I congratulated her, she lost control and fell. A little deterred from continuing, she said to me exasperatedly and with a deep sigh, "Momma, can you just stay in the kitchen and don't look, okay?" I smiled and turned around as I continued with dinner preparations.

After some time had passed, she asked me to stand toward the bar to watch her go down the hallway again. I cautiously turned to her with a smile and watched her wobble right past me. Her hands gripped the handle bar tightly; her bright eyes gazed over the front of her bike looking downward at the handle and front tire trying with all her might to keep upright and pedaling at the same time. I wanted to cheer for her but kept quiet hoping not to distract her. When she came back up the hallway, she ran into the wall just short of the bar where I stood. Infuriated and tired, she dropped her bike and leaned up against the wall with her arms folded tightly across her chest. Her little lips were poked out as far as they could go, and her keen chin was tucked into her chest. A fountain of tears then came down and made a stream down her cheeks. I purposely stayed away so she could come to a resolve on her own, but discreetly watched her grow tired of standing until she slid her back down the wall and hit the floor in a slouched position, arms still folded and all. I chuckled to myself thinking how cute she was. She probably sat there about five minutes pouting — then it was time for dinner. When I asked her to put her bike away she cried out, begging for one more chance to try. Since she had wasted time sulking, I took the bike away but encouraged her; she almost had it under control, and I promised we would resume practicing the next evening.

As soon as we arrived home the next evening, I grabbed the bike and we went outside to continue with her lessons. To my surprise, she hopped on immediately even though I asked her to wait a second until she pushed it to the sidewalk because our front yard has a small downward slope towards the street. She insisted, so I let her have the bike, and, like a champ, she got on it and pedaled across the street. She yelled, "Look momma, I'm riding, I'm riding!" We stayed out for a long time while she rode; she turned to me and said, "This is so easy momma." I laughed because I knew once she conquered her fear of falling, the skill would develop effortlessly. She has been riding without my help since then.

This experience was so rewarding for me. I thoroughly enjoyed every bit of watching our little girl learn how to ride her bike. Some moments were indeed frustrating for her and a little disheartening for me from a parent's view. Standing back watching her fall countless times were difficult, but witnessing her dedication and hard work made it all worthwhile. It amazes me that when you are about God's business and developing an intimate relationship with him, you see him everywhere and in everything — great or small. Hannah had been begging for a while to learn how to ride her bike, but it did not happen until she picked it up and tried to ride it. I could have hoped for her and she could have continued to hope, but the blessing did not occur and would not have occurred until she added a little work to her faith.

Standing in the shadows watching her, I repositioned myself and pictured our Heavenly Father as the parent and me as his child journeying through life. You see, our father sometimes allows just enough space to keep a watchful eye on us, but is always readily available when we call out to him for help (Psalm 46:1, kjv). There are also times when he purposely allows us to fall over and over again to help us develop certain skills to learn things on our own. As the picture became clearer in my mind, I held back tears of joy. I know if my father feels as much joy and love as I do for my child when she accomplishes anything, or merely because I am her mom, I know how deep his love is for me, his child.

During the times Hannah became frustrated to the point where she would drop her bike and wanted to stop, the mom in me wanted to step in so badly, but out of love I left her alone. Sometimes when I also feel frustrated and want to give up, I have to remind myself that I am not alone — even when I feel like God has abandoned me. I know I have a father who cares for me and loves me unconditionally. He is always near, waiting for the perfect time to step in and take control over situations that are too big for me to handle on my own. At other times, he stands on the sideline. He congratulates me when I get up from a hard fall and cheers me on as I continue taking one more step towards accomplishing my goals. The most valuable part of helping Hannah learn how to ride her bike was I really didn't help her. She applied work to faith; she expected to ride her bike all by herself and she did. When faith is present, fear disappears. She learned a lesson of faith.

"Even so faith, if it hath not works, is dead being alone."

(James 2:17, KJV)

Storms of Life
Come and Go

Let's face it, all of us have encountered and weath-ered some type of storm during the course of our lives. It may have been a thunderstorm, rainstorm, hurricane, tornado, or blizzard, but the fact of the matter is that as bad as we may recoil from breaking news of adverse weather, it is a necessary part of life just like everything else aligned with God's beautiful creation and magnificent plans.

Although the comparison of life and environ-mental storms are strong, life's storms do not consist of drenching and flooding rains, but heartache; no gale force strong wind gusts, but loss; no sharp-striking lightening, but tears, confusion, and difficulties.

During some of life's most horrific storms, some families experience loss, and destruction—homes that were newly built or in good condition are now ruined, run down, and dilapidated. Some may have even experienced complete loss where the owners must relocate to allow time for renovation. The truth is: no one wants to experience life-threatening or life-changing storms, but they do come. How will you handle them or prepare?

With the aid of highly technological equipment, weather forecasters are able to communicate swiftly, accurately, and efficiently to send bulletins through TV and radio stations to warn those along a storm's pathway. Many times the warnings come days in advance, which gives communities notice to either equip themselves to ride out the storm or vacate the area until it passes. Notice the word *passes*. It does eventually pass! However, there have been occasions where environmental storms hit without notice or warning. Sadly, those are the kind that usually leave catastrophic loss and devastation, which is also true for life storms.

The key to surviving any storm is that you not wait until it is predicted to hit, but to prepare in advance even if it never strikes. Preparation. Who or what will determine whether you have made preparations? There is a saying that goes; "Only the strong survive." That is true to a degree, but I would like to also add "Only the strong and well-prepared survive."

Will you be like the disciples on the ship with Jesus who feared they were going to perish (Matthew 8:23 — 27, KJV)? Who or what is your foundation built upon? My preparation is stronger and more powerful than any storm. He can withstand even the most torrential waves, winds, and rains; he can carry me in the midst of what forecasters predict to be catastrophic. He has not only carried me, but comforted me, and has given me peace in the midst of my troubles — Jesus! Even when I am not in the midst of a storm he sits with me, uplifts me, talks with me, listens to me, comforts me, corrects me (when I am wrong), and helps me throughout each and every single day. If you invite him, he can very well carry you through any situation, big or small.

There have been a few times when I'd rather stay in bed rather than prepare for work or my day, simply to lay in bed and meditate on God's holy word. The times that I take my eyes off of God for a split second is when I find myself wanting to quit. Those are the moments God cheers me on and gives me hope to keep going — he doesn't allow me to quit.

One winter morning, I recall waking up, not well at all, but I still had to get up to take Hannah to school. I was not feeling well at all—a thunderstorm was brewing. I laid there snug in my bed, with the covers pulled nearly all the way over my head with only my hair sticking through to allow airflow underneath the covers, thinking, "If I can just get up, I will make it through the day." I pushed myself up to my feet and walked slowly into Hannah's bathroom down the hallway from my bedroom. When I flipped on the lights the first thing I saw was the drawing she had painted in preschool about five years ago, hanging over her toilet. It was a butterfly designed from her small handprints with splashes of other bright colors painted in the background. She had used the tips of her tiny fingers and palms of her hand to design the painting. The butterfly wings of her handprints shined through like a bright light. All the other colors became hope to me as I envisioned how much fun it must have been for her to play in all the finger paint to make that drawing for us. I snickered, holding back tears of solace and said to Jesus, "Thank you so much." I was ready for my workday and the rest of my week; got myself together, stood strong and tall knowing who was in charge of my life and me. He had been in charge even when I found myself too discouraged to begin my day. That morning he had calmed the brewing thunderstorm in its tracks, headed straight towards me. He reminded me where the root of happiness truly comes from and the innocence life offers us on a daily basis. I got up with God's help as he continued to carry me.

My perspective shifted from thinking about how badly I felt to positive things, and how if we try to control our thoughts through adversity and place our focus on God we will be able to see all of the beautiful paintings before us that go unnoticed. You see, we are not perfect, but with God on our side, we can make it — learn, grow, and become better, stronger individuals. Allow him to be your foundation so that you, too, can withstand some of life's storms.

"And when he was entered into a ship, his disciples followed him. And, behold, there arose a great tempest in the sea, insomuch that the ship was covered with the waves: but he was asleep. And his disciples came to him, and awoke him, saying, Lord, save us: we perish. And he saith unto them, Why are ye fearful, O ye of little faith? Then he arose, and rebuked the winds and the sea; and there was a great calm. But the men marveled, saying, what manner of man is this, that even the winds and the sea obey him!"

(Matthew 8:23 — 27, KJV)

All of a Sudden...

Do you ever hear people respond to situations by asking, "Why did this happen all of a sudden?" When I hear this in the form of a question or statement, my radar goes off, because I personally do not believe most things happen *all of a sudden* unless there is a mighty move of God. God's power is infinite and can be instantaneous when he chooses. I do also believe there are tragic situations that really do occur without warning or notice. However, when something happens to shake or distress an individual, relationship, community, etc. there are usually premature warning signs prior to the unveiling. In life, there is always a beginning, a middle, and an end to everything regardless how short or long-lived. Nine times out of ten, from my perspective, nothing in life suddenly occurs except by the mighty move of God.

I recall a time my husband and I watched the movie—*Fire Proof,* which by the way is an awesome movie about fire proofing your marriage. After watching the movie, I brought up conversations about how small fires have just as much an impact on a marriage as the large fires, and pointed out some of our small fires. We disagreed. Not recognizing a fire regardless of its size is the reason one can refer to life changing events such as separation and divorce, as happening "all of a sudden".

Sometimes people say, "All of a sudden she or he changed on me." Does anyone change overnight? Is that even possible? I don't think so. What I believe occurs is that people ignore the early warning signs until it is too late and become blind to what is truly happening around them. When it becomes too late or almost too late to respond to problems is the time when you will hear *all of a sudden* …

I remember my mother used to always say, "You have to watch as well as pray." One of the ways things crumble before our eyes is that we sometimes fail to pay attention to our surroundings. We fail to listen, and we fail to see all of the answers provided to us on a daily basis. When things go terribly wrong, many want to blame someone else for the real problems at hand. When will we learn to take responsibility for our own actions or non-actions? When will we learn to accept that we made a mistake or acknowledge when we are wrong and humbly admit it?

If we want answers to the question, "why all of a sudden?" we must first humbly seek God and turn to his holy word. Second, step back away from the situation and press the rewind button in your mind to see what you may have missed; be assured you will find that you indeed missed some crucial things. Third, open your eyes and ears and start paying attention. Failing to pay attention is the first step to failure or loss. Finally, lose self-centeredness. Did you know that when you are selfish in the slightest way, it is hard to see anyone else's needs other than yours?

If a problem occurs in your life, please understand its seed was planted. Once planted, little by little, it will produce fruit by the nourishment of your actions or non-actions. Before long, what wasn't recognized as a negative seed is now showing its ugly face, a poisonous plant. How destructive or how much damage that plant causes depends upon how much is consumed. We must come to fully understand that negative and destructive seeds produce a harvest just as well as positive seeds.

God *always* provides an answer even when it isn't the answer you prefer or what you want to hear. He tells us when to start and when to stop. I don't know about you, but I put my confidence and trust in him enough to go with his answers, even when they do not make a bit of sense to me at the time.

"My People are destroyed for lack of knowledge."

(Hosea 4:6, KJV)

Understanding Your Roles

We play many roles in life, but all of those roles are (I would hope) still a part of who we are. Whether assigned, voluntary, or by birth, they all carry levels of responsibility which holds us accountable for our actions.

Realistically speaking, we must also take time to study and seek Godly wisdom to fulfill our roles, which were designed by God (Jeremiah 29:11, KJV). In order to be or remain successful in our life stories, we must first understand what God requires of us in order to play the part he designed for us. As a little girl, I watched my mom switch many roles, while sometimes playing different roles simultaneously. She was outstanding in some, and in others she had difficulty. Sometimes her roles were hard to balance and caused some conflict, but as a mother and wife — to name a few — she was a wonderful nurturer and giver. She was the one person I knew who truly understood sacrifice. Because she understood sacrifice, her character was guided into a loving, nurturing, and giving individual, which was felt by many.

One reason relationships fail is because people do not take the time to seek Godly wisdom, and thus understand their roles. A wife cannot take on the character to be her husband's mother and a husband cannot take on the character of a father to his wife. God specifically designed each role for very specific reasons, and if you do not understand your role, you may have unnecessary controversy and conflict. In like manner, a parent cannot take the role of a best buddy or pal with their children. Parents should be held to a degree of reverence. In a business, the director or president cannot be best buddies or pals with their employees.

I see so many hurting individuals, companies, and relationships simply because of a lack of understanding. Once people know what their roles require of them, they should be able to transcend into that person and become the best they can be. Before accepting a role — husband, wife, employee, or friend, decide realistically if you are able to perform and handle the responsibilities that come along with it. If not, swallow your pride and be honest with yourself and others. Nobody is perfect, but if you seek God, put forth great effort, and understand what your role requires, your relationships will flourish.

If we as a society can begin to understand this, there will be more successful businesses, happier and healthier families, communities — and yes — a better world.

> "Wherefore comfort yourselves together, and edify one another, even as also ye do."
>
> (1Thessalonians 5:11, KJV)

Let's Take a Walk

Have you ever prayed, "Lord, bless my family;" "Lord, bless them in a mighty way;" or "Lord, keep them and be with them"? I pray this way often for friends, family, coworkers, our national leaders, and even for myself. Well, as I was driving down the highway and talking with the Lord one night, the words "Just think back, Sonya" filled my thoughts. "Think about each day you are alive; moving from morning through mid-day, then evening to bedtime." All those moments, are times that you are kept by the hand of God. As I went on my way to meet friends for a social outing, I was seeking guidance about a situation.

The phrase—'*Lord, bless*' drowned my thoughts as I began reflecting on previous difficulties encountered, and eventually, overcome throughout my life. At that moment, a series of scenes from my past flashed before me as if someone was rewinding and fast forwarding my life.

When I was a little girl around the age of nine or so, I would sit down in the dirt and draw pictures of my future house and future family. It was a time when I had so many hopes and dreams. Now, as a young woman, I am still very hopeful and ambitious, and although I am not drawing my plans and goals in the dirt, I am drawing them in my mind and jotting down the details on paper.

I recalled one time I said to the Lord: "Lord, bless me *beyond* my greatest dream and expand my territory."

Then the Lord really tapped into my heart. "But Sonya, I am already doing that."

The rewind button was pushed again; I had to say, "Yes, Lord, you are so right." The Lord knows what we all need each and every single day, every minute and hour. He already knows our purposes and our destinies and sees far beyond our today and tomorrow. Instead of praying for what we think we need or for what we don't have, just simply praise him. God has already taken care of us in advance.

As a teenager, my greatest dream was to graduate from high school, go to college, and have a family. Guess what? God provided a way for me to do just that. Back then, when I was aspiring to have all of those things, they seemed so far off and unreachable which, ironically, is what kept me reaching.

I recall my senior year of high school, when my guidance counselor told me in a serious tone, looking down over her glasses, that I was not college material. What a lie that was — not only did I go to college, but I graduated with honors. I also recall my doctor telling me that the possibility of my having a successful full-term pregnancy without being on bed rest was slim. Although Hannah was born premature at twenty-seven weeks, and weighed a little over two pounds, she is here and healthy.

In reflecting back, there were times I wasn't even sure how I could afford a car or a home, but with the help of God, I have those things also. So you see, after a brief journey down memory lane, not only do I realize that God has blessed me far beyond what I have dreamed, but also he has continued to keep me and help me this far in life. God continues to take us higher, even through struggles.

At each new phase in my life or at each new crossroad in my life, not only does my vision multiply, but through it all — the good and the bad, it equates to a desire to live a life that is more pleasing to my God. I'm realizing that I do not have to beg

God for anything, but just be thankful, because in my believing he is blessing me each and every day.

As I continue my walk with the Lord—ambitious, full of visions and aspirations, I know God is well capable of opening new doors of opportunity in my life. He will bring the visions, drawn in my mind, to life. I will be that successful author, business owner, devoted and phenomenal woman God has called me to be.

Today, as you read this story, instead of praying, "Lord, bless me and help me to get this or that," go ahead and thank him in advance for the blessings that are coming, as well as those you have already received. If you do not believe that he can bless you in advance, take a walk back into the past, and then fast forward to now and tell me what you find.

I have been blessed beyond some of my greatest dreams. You can also continue to walk in hope and keep those dreams alive because God is not finished with his special creation—You. Glorify him and honor his precious name. With God, all things are possible to those who believe and are willing to work.

> "And Jesus looking upon them saith, With men it is impossible, but not with God: for with God all things are possible"
>
> (Mark 10:27, KJV)

I'm Invisible,
But Can You See Me?

I passed a breathtaking scene as I drove home from work one evening. As I approached this scene, I slowed my car down to the point where I almost came to a complete stop. Traffic was moving steadily behind me so I had to continue driving along. This scene was so tranquil, beautiful, and graceful that I turned my car around and stopped on the side of the road and just sat there in awe.

On this particular day, while sitting in my car by the side of the road, I could clearly see God through his magnificent creations. I saw the clear blue sky and everything within its space. I knew I had to pick Hannah up from school, but for that moment, I was captivated. I sat there looking up and around—I saw the clear blue sky, the rustic beauty of the old silos, and the entire scene before me. It reminded me of a song titled "Invisible" by Jennifer Hudson. In her lyrics, she sings a verse, "can you see me?" Those words touch my soul deeply because most of the time we have all we need right before our very eyes but our attention is shifted elsewhere and many of our blessings go unnoticed and unappreciated. However, in this moment, I could see vividly. I truly saw the face of God, and I wanted so badly to share it with my loved ones. I observed his marvelous creation of the boundless skies; the warm sun beaming in on the crisp, chilled, fall evening; and the array of trees that had just started to turn colors. I could even see the small, white house across from the silos and thought, "Man! The individual or family who lives there is so blessed." Did you catch that—*blessed?* The house was not a mansion on an exotic island in Barbados or Jamaica; rather, it was located off a country road in Raleigh, North Carolina. This small, white wooden farmhouse was surrounded by huge, shady trees on many acres of land, which to me was priceless. One may view that very scene and wonder what my amazement is all about—the house was surrounded by such beauty; how could it go unnoticed? Although God is invisible, I can see Him. Can you?

This was an *eyes-of-a-child* moment. I think about how we, as adults, are so busy that we miss out on so much. We miss embracing simplicity and true beauty. Through the eyes of my eight-year-old daughter, Hannah, my sense of seeing and hearing has sharpened tremendously. Practically every morning that I take her to school, she sees or hears something. I do not notice it because I am either rushing to get out of the house so we can be on time, or my mind is clouded with so many other things that need my attention. There have been many times when she, out of excitement and awe, yelled to me, "Mommy, look at that!" It could be a bird, a tree, or anything. Sadly, had she not brought those things to my attention, I would have missed it. We miss out on so many blessings; too often, we miss the joy of hearing and seeing God.

Since becoming a mother, I pay more attention to things; especially the beauty of God's creations. Hannah points out things on a daily basis that I would normally miss. Even as a baby, she would gaze at things around her and although she could not talk, her laughter and cooing would always turn my attention to what she was observing. Now that she is older I still listen to her thrill of discovery all the time; that is one of my daily blessings. Seeing through her eyes of discovery gives me a sense of peace and humility that I am in God's presence all of the time. Her excitement of discovery causes me to see from a different perspective — instead of seeing a bird, I see God's bird! In awe, my heart fills with thankfulness because when I now look around in my own surroundings, I see the glory of God in every-thing — large and small. Sometimes, as we age, we tend to lose the innocence of observance — observing the simple, yet powerful things that cause us to see God's magnificent power.

> "The earth is the LORD's, and the fullness thereof; the world, and they that dwell therein."
>
> (Psalm 24:1, KJV)

I'm a Wildflower Child

While sitting at my computer one lovely Sunday night, smiling and humbly striking my keyboard, I was looking into my monitor with free thoughts flowing through my mind. My heart was feeling so overwhelmingly loved, and at peace. If I had to describe my heart at that moment, I would ask you to envision a field of wildflowers — the red, purple, and yellow ones you see while driving along the highways, at least in North Carolina.

It happened to be Mother's Day weekend. For a long time since her passing, I felt completely free, and totally content. Of course, I miss spending Mother's Day, and every day with Mom, but I let her go. Hannah and Julian had gone fishing to give me some time to myself, and instead of going out shopping or doing other things I enjoy, I simply took time to reflect. As I thought about my mother that weekend, I felt her love and presence as I envisioned a field of wildflowers. While on earth, she shared her heart far and wide through her words of encouragement, her smile, and all of her warm hugs.

I have always, always loved wildflowers because they not only grow freely by the dozens, but they are beautiful. I have shared with Julian from time to time how I would love to plant wildflowers all along the perimeters of our home. I'm sure he thinks I'm crazy sometimes, but I'm so serious about that. While the average homeowner carefully picks out seasonal flowers with fresh mulch and decorate their flowerbeds, I simply want wildflowers. I didn't realize there were so many different types of wildflowers until I did a little research — wow! What I love most about them is how they look like weeds with pretty colors on the top of them. On some beautiful sunny days, as I'm driving to see family and friends, I am so tempted to pull over and spread out a blanket and have a picnic lunch right beside the highway in the midst of the wildflowers. There's just something about them that spells freedom to me.

As a child, I would compare myself to many things, from a rabbit to a squirrel and yes, even flowers. I guess comparing myself to a wildflower isn't too far fetched for me because I really am wild, in spirit and heart — similar to my mom. I'm no ordinary chick, that's for sure. I like to spread myself as wide and as far as I possibly can go and grow. I know I am only one person, but spreading yourself doesn't require you to be on a plane traveling all throughout the week, in several places over the course of a day, week or month. It simply means, in my opinion, to give of yourself freely, tapping into your purpose and being the blessing God intended you to be.

I am truly blessed beyond my wildest imagination. The gift of spreading yourself like wildflowers to others from all walks of life is that you receive the best gift in return. People give their hearts back to you. I've seen an email that circulates from time to time that says, "Some people are for a reason, a season, or a lifetime." I believe that is so true, and I also believe whether for a reason, season, or lifetime" they are all blessings. During the course of Mother's Day Week 2009, I was blessed with many people who also extended themselves like wildflowers and what a blessing they were to me. Although my mother is no longer here, I have been blessed with other mothers, of my friends, who care for me. They call to check on me during the week and I do the same. They also represent wildflowers because they take the time to share their heartfelt care and concern with me. I appreciate and love them dearly for that.

God has truly blessed me with several people who I can honestly say care about me. I truly believe when someone gives from the depth of his or her heart, the gift is everlasting. Look at what God did for each of us when he gave his son, Jesus, from the depth of his heart. Jesus is definitely a lifetime gift and he certainly always has a reason and a season for positioning people into our lives. I cannot say who is in my life for one reason or another, or whether they will be in my life for a short period of time or an extended period. One thing I am certain, if God took the time to place them into my life for whatever reason, when he did, then they are my blessing — yesterday, today, and tomorrow. Even if that relationship wasn't as close as some of my other relationships, or did not last, it does not matter. What does matter is the one who gave life to the relationship, at his perfect time, for his benefit. I guess being a wildflower child isn't so bad after all.

"For, brethren, ye have been called unto liberty; only use not liberty for an occasion to the flesh, but by love serve one another."

(Galatians 5:13, KJV)

It's Just an Earthworm

I had gotten up early one Sunday morning to go for a walk/run around the high school track, not far from my home. Whenever I go for a jog or walk outside, I always take my time during my first lap to absorb my surroundings and indulge all of my senses in God's magnificent creations.

I arrived at the track around seven thirty in the morning. There was a slight chill in the air, apparently from the cold front that came along with the showers throughout the night. The only way I could tell it had rained was from the dampness of the ground. The sun was up and the sky was clear blue with only a few clouds. It was the perfect morning for a jog.

I had walked perhaps a few yards when I noticed an earthworm wiggling its way across the track. For a short second I wondered, "How in the world did he get on this track?" My thoughts swiftly left the worm and shifted on to something different and I began praising God for His miracles, this day. I had clocked a quarter of a mile and decided to pick up my speed, preparing myself to start jogging, but just as I began to start, I noticed the worm had wiggled his way over from one side of the track to the middle. It's amazing how seeing that earthworm had turned into a blessing that morning and also became my motivation and encouragement to jog when I really wanted to stop.

Into my fourth lap, I didn't see the worm. All I remembered was he was headed toward the football field, which was positioned on the inside of the track. The football field was an environment where he could have survived — a manicured lawn with rich soil underneath it. Had he not gotten to the soil in time, the sun would have killed him during his journey towards his desired destination. I thought back to the many times when I have seen dead earthworms lying on sidewalks and in various places. Those were the select few that didn't make it and couldn't find soil in time to survive. The elements of the unfamiliar environment, such as the sun, had killed them. That thought pushed me to run and walk more than I had initially planned to do.

In life, there may be times that we find ourselves in unfamiliar territory—away from our comfort zones. The unfamiliar elements can either serve as our opponent or our fuel to press even harder toward a goal. I have seen dead worms lying on the pavement after a rainy day, which was followed by sunshine. The elements of opposition, in their case, were too difficult to bear. Although unfamiliar, we, too, must always press our way towards that Promised Land that God has already set before us.

If we can change our mindset to give it our all, to be purpose driven to do things God's way instead of our own way, then we can be a witness to those around us. There is some truth to the saying "What does not kill you, will make you stronger." We also can survive and possess the land as that worm did that day on the track. Had he not pressed his way towards that field, I'm not sure if he would have survived but, lay dead on the ground, like some of the other worms.

This reflection helped me to realize that I must continue to strive to do better in all areas of my life. Regardless of the unfamiliar situations that lie before me, I know that God has already set the land before me and all I have to do is possess it. Go and possess your land!

> "And I said unto you, ye are come unto the mountain of the Amorites, which the LORD our God doth give unto us. 21: Behold, the LORD thy God hath set the land before thee: go up and possess it, as the LORD God of thy fathers hath said unto thee; fear not, neither be discouraged."
>
> (Deuteronomy 1: 20 — 21, KJV)

Innocence Lost

Our date had gone really well. I was feeling so beautiful and special to him after all the compliments he showered on me over the course of the evening. I had always been a fool for nature and loved spending time outdoors, so his suggestion to take a walk at the park, after leaving the theater, sounded like a wonderful idea. We sat on the park bench gazing into each other's eyes. The brightness of the moon beamed in the clear night sky, and reflected onto our faces from the water in the swimming pool. "You are so beautiful and I am so lucky to have you here with me right now. Do you know how long I've waited for this moment?" he said.

Blushing, in a shy manner, I smiled and shook my head no. My heart melted as he gently stroked my face with his strong hands, guiding me towards him for a kiss. I hesitated a little by pulling back and removing his hand from my face, not wanting to rush the night away. Instead of pulling me back, he moved his body closer to me, and gently took my hand, and placed it onto his face. He did not say a word, but his eyes told me everything I needed to know—he wanted to kiss me badly. Finally, I answered him with my eyes, giving him the okay to kiss me, and we shared a short kiss. "That was nice." I said with a smile. Satisfied with that one kiss, I started to stand up because I felt a little uncomfortable. Things had gone great so far, and it was our second date, but I simply did not want to rush things.

As I stood to my feet, turning my back to him, he met me, stepping from behind and holding me by the waist. He said some other nice things to me, but not wanting to show how uncomfortable I was, I just smiled at his remarks about how fantastic I looked. Totally taking me off guard, he grabbed me and kissed me passionately. At that point I felt okay—a little uncomfortable, but okay. He knew I did not care to be in confined places and suffered from mild claustrophobia. When he continued holding me too close, I resisted a bit, but did not say anything and continued to let him hold and caress me. Things were happening way too fast and I tried to push him away, but he wouldn't let go. That is when I felt threatened.

Quickly glancing around the slightly lit area, with total darkness all around the park bench, I hoped we were not alone near the huge tree. I thought, *this cannot be happening to me.* I squirmed, trying to break free as his strong arms tightened around my body. I could not get away. It was weird how the kisses I thought had been so sweet and endearing, became nasty and unattractive. I'm sure I must have said no a hundred times, but he did not listen. My no's seemed to have spelled yes, and the more I told him no the more aggressive he became. The night I considered to be a great date turned into my worst nightmare. I can say it now: date rape. I trusted this man enough to go on a date with him more than once; I even enjoyed his kisses and his touch at one point. How could I dislike him all so suddenly?

I remember the drive home that night, clinging to the passenger door with all my might and sitting with my legs closed so tight they hurt. I prayed that he wouldn't reach over to touch me or look at me. Finally, we made it back to my place where I almost fell to the ground exiting his car just to be free of him. Although I never looked into his eyes again, I remembered that grimacing look of frustration and anger on his face for a long, long time. I guess I really did not know him after all.

A question I asked myself for a long time is 'why did I allow this to happen?' Instead of talking about what happened to me, over the years, I went into protective mode and vowed I wouldn't let it happen ever again. I built a wall that kept me from trusting anyone, even those who genuinely cared about me. Next, came the wall of fear that always kept me on my guard. A lack of trust and fear will destroy progress and relationships. Fear alone stops you dead in your tracks; everything and everyone becomes a suspect.

A lot of times, bad experiences and baggage will keep us from receiving our blessings. We wonder why we are not being blessed, why our relationships fail, and why everything around us seems so wrong. However, the irony of it all is not everything around us is wrong; we are wrong and we become our worst enemy and critic.

Over the course of our lives, we put up so many walls—distrust, fear, pride, and so on. However, building those walls does not protect us nor stop attacks from happening to us. Instead, we become our own enemy and attack ourselves. We hold ourselves captive behind our own walls. Sounds crazy, huh? Think about it. Has anyone ever hurt you and you said you would never, ever allow anyone to hurt you that way again? Automatically, you go on the defense and you don't let anything in or come near you. The purpose of a defense line in any sport is to stop the opposition. Who is your opposing team? Your family and friends — those closest to you?

When we are on the defense, day in and day out, we rob ourselves and stop the intended flow of our blessings. Although it may appear we have a strong defense strategy and are winning, we really are losing out in the game of life.

I allowed that man to stop me for a long time. But I finally let it all go and have torn down all those unnecessary walls that became strongholds over me. I pray he will never hurt another woman the way he hurt me. I realized I was hurting myself in so many ways by holding on to those painful memories of date rape. Over time, I forgave myself for what I thought was my fault at the time, being careless and irresponsible. I also have forgiven him for not realizing the depth of physical and mental pain he caused me.

One may question how I could forgive him for doing what he did to me. I desperately wanted to move past my feelings of hurt, guilt, fear, resentment and anger, so I sought God like I never have before. I did not want to carry that weight around with me, which robbed me of my happiness and freedom. Therefore, over a time of steadfast prayer, and holding on to my faith, God began to heal me. Little by little, and day by day, I was delivered as I spent time in prayer and it increased my faith. I still think about it once and a while, but it no longer engulfs me with fear or make me ashamed of myself for what happened that dreadful night. I was finally free.

"Say not thou, I will recompense evil; but wait on the LORD, and he shall save thee."

(Proverbs 20:22, KJV)

If the Son therefore shall make you free, ye shall be free indeed.

(John 8:36, KJV)

Daddy's Gift

There is something charming, giddy, and special to a little girl when her daddy loves, encourages, and fights for her. Although I was blessed to have my dad in my life until he passed away, in June 2000, we didn't become close until I got older.

Over time, after leaving home to attend college, my focus and appreciation shifted. I began to talk to Dad more, and shared stories about my college experiences with him. I could tell he missed me when I was away. He was always happy to see me when I came home during holiday or summer breaks.

I recall this story often, when I think about my dad—I was seven or eight-years-old. It was a hot summer day when Dad gave me the cutest little rubber puppy. He was white with brownish orange spots and black droopy-looking ears. I adored him, and cherished him more than my baby dolls because *my daddy* bought him especially for me. I always had him with me in my arms everywhere I went. About a few weeks after I got him, Dad carried Tonya, Tony, and I with him fishing. We eagerly and excitedly jumped on the back of his old Ford pickup truck. It was rusty orange with white stripes — the coolest truck ever. It also had the loudest muffler around town, which is why I loved it.

On our way to the pond to go fishing, I sat on the back of the truck as happy as a bee in a patch of honeysuckles. The brisk, cool breeze swept across my face, and through the scalp of my braided hair as I enjoyed our long ride to the pond. It was an enjoyable trip — the three of us sat facing each other, riding down the country roads. As we crossed a bridge, Tonya reached over and grabbed my puppy out of my arms, without notice or warning. I screamed abruptly. Dad looked back at us through his rear view mirror. He did not stop to see why I was screaming because we fought and argued about everything. It was not out of the norm to hear either of us yelling or screaming at each other. Dad continued driving down the road. Before I could reach to grab my puppy back from Tonya, she tossed him off the truck and over the bridge — he fell into the river. My heart sank; I retaliated by punching and kicking Tonya. This time, Dad had no choice but to stop. He pulled his truck over on side of the road in the downtown area of Snow Hill. In a panic, crying uncontrollably, and unable to speak clearly, I managed to tell Dad that Tonya had tossed my puppy over the bridge. She was in big trouble! Although she was disciplined for her mean act, we never found my puppy.

The special part about this story was the love displayed through the gift my father gave me — my puppy. I remember the disappointing look in his eyes when he realized Tonya had thrown my puppy over the bridge and he didn't know how to calm me down. We did not go to the pond that day, but the drive back home, sitting inside the truck with him is a memory I cherish and have carried in my heart. I sat next to him with my head under the pit of his arm. While I sniffed and wiped tears away from my eyes, he glanced down at me and told me *everything would be okay.* At that point, although I was upset that my puppy was gone, I calmed down and stopped crying. I knew if he could, Dad would have bought me a hundred puppies to replace that *one.*

Although there was a gap where Dad and I were not as close, that memory counts for several special moments — all wrapped into one gift. What gift do you value? Can you recall a time that you received a special gift from someone? Our Heavenly Father has given you an invaluable gift. It cannot be thrown away or snatched out of our hands — it belongs to you through your faith. Every day you are alive, God's gift remains available to you — it belongs to you if you desire it.

> "Like as a father pitieth his children, so the Lord pitieth them that fear him."
>
> (Psalm 103:13, KJV)

The Skin You're In

I've heard the slogan, "Love the skin you're in" from Oil of Olay's™ beauty campaign. It also reminds me of the Dove slogan — I'm sure you have heard it as well. Boy, do I love Dove's™ soap and body wash, but I don't think of soap or its claim of smoother and healthier skin when I hear that slogan. I do, however, think of who tailor-made my skin to fit me. Regardless of your color or creed, the root of who you are is not determined by your skin's outer appearance, but what is beneath it. It is your heart and who you choose to become.

For me, I can honestly say my skin doesn't define me, and I so love the skin God chose for me. Not only did he create it, but also created every defining detail that makes me unique and 'plain ole me'. He even chose my parents to create me for His specific purpose. He is my sole source of existence — my every breath, and I thirst and hunger for him. Because he lives within me, it should not matter about the skin I'm in.

Through God's all powerful and unchanging hands, he has blessed me to have life and to have it more abundantly; I am so thankful every day for every family member and every ancestor and for friends that paved the way to get me to this point. I am even thankful for my enemies; they have helped to make me a better person. In him is where I put my trust, and in him, I am made whole with a loving, humble, and sincere heart committed to giving and being the best I can to help others along life's journey. I am so thankful for the skin he put me in.

So I say to you — from my heart to yours — love the skin you're in, not because of Dove™ or Oil of Olay™, but because God put you in it. For you, too, are fearfully and wonderfully made for his purpose.

> "I will praise thee; for I am fearfully and wonderfully made: marvellous are thy works; and that my soul knoweth right well."
>
> (Psalm 139:14, KJV)

God created and called you

to have life and live more abundantly

not to live in the shadows of others

but to embrace your uniqueness and discover your own identity

Never feel ashamed of who you are -

though your skin may be different

you are still a child of God

not a mistake, a duplicate or misprint.

— S L Hackett

Remembering

All people share one thing in common; missing loved ones who have passed away and have gone on to be with the Lord. For me, although it has been over ten years since my mom passed, I still miss her dearly. When you lose someone you love and hold near and dear to your heart, it changes your life in a profound way. Grieving comes and goes, but you never, ever forget special people who truly touched and changed your life.

Losing my mother was the hardest because it was almost like someone kidnapped her from me (us) in the middle of the night and never brought her back. Ironically, someone did, but not maliciously. God took her home. She passed away so suddenly in the early morning hours, without notice. I knew she was not well, suffering with high blood pressure and some other things, but did not know she was ill enough to die. She did not like going to the doctor at all. I could not find immediate closure because initially, I did not know the cause of her death.

Since losing loved ones, the one thing that has changed is my personal perspective on life. I don't take anything or anyone for granted. I seize the moments and treasure what I have in family and friends. There are times when I may very well be tired or I may not feel like reading that special book with Hannah or sitting up a few minutes later to chit chat with Julian. However, in that one second when I could selfishly think only of myself and choose to do something else that really won't matter a day, a week, or a year from now, I'm tossing away precious memories that may very well matter to them one day.

I think about the last day with my mother. I didn't know this until much later, but she did not feel well enough to travel and visit us, but she decided to spend it with my family anyway. She chose to put aside thoughts of selfishness and pity. I think back on that day how I shared with her my hopes of becoming a mother and showed her which room I was considering for our baby's room, when the time came.

I recall looking into her eyes—I remember how proud she was of us. I got to hold her hand, and sit, and talk with her. Had she said, "You know, Sonya I just don't feel like taking the trip today", she would have never gotten to experience seeing me excited about purchasing our first home. I would have never experienced having my own mother over to eat at my house. I am so glad that she came and shared that day with us. Because she loved me, she chose not to focus on how she felt nor did she complain. If she had complained, I would have asked her to stay home simply out of my love and concern for her. However, she was right where she wanted to be and I love her dearly for teaching me how to give unselfishly, to love wholeheartedly, and how to be a genuine woman of God.

If you knew today was going to be your last day, to what and to whom would you say no? How important are the people in your life that you say you love, but put off spending time with for one reason or another? I am not suggesting you stop every single thing and fall at their feet, but sometimes, the moments that seem so insignificant are the ones that leave everlasting memories.

Although she is no longer here, I have that one last day of memories with her and I feel so much joy. My mother always wanted to be able to buy us the finer things in life and invest money into our future so we wouldn't have to struggle as she did. However, the greatest gift she ever gave and shared with me wasn't anything of monetary value. My mother taught me about the only one who could give me everything I need — peace, love, and happiness — Jesus Christ, my Lord and personal savior. He is the greatest gift I ever received.

> "Blessed are they that mourn: for they shall be comforted."
>
> (Matthew 5:4, KJV)

I Have a Surprise for You

It was pouring rain and my friend, Tee, and I drove for two hours to Mooresville, North Carolina; it was a trip we both dreaded. We had to go — although she and I dreaded the long drive, we knew our presence was needed.

The week prior to our trip, I received the heart-wrenching phone call from Leigh, a friend of mine that one of our friends, Keyna, had passed away suddenly. We all talked off and on during the week approaching the funeral, offering support to one another and preparing ourselves to be as supportive as we could to Keyna's family. Our pain could not compare to what they were feeling at this time of the unexpected death of their child.

The one thing I remember about Keyna is that she would always share devotional books and CDs of sermons with me; whether they came from her church or if she purchased them. Her enthusiasm towards spiritual growth was astounding. In particular, I recall not long after meeting her as one of my roommates in college, she gave me a tape of a sermon entitled, *Why are you so Fearful* by Pastor Gool. I must have played that tape a thousand times — it changed my life for the better by understanding fear, which helped me to learn how to stand stronger in my faith. After listening to the tape a few times I said to her, "I have to go to his church and hear him preach."

At the funeral, while sitting on the front row reserved for the flower girls during her funeral, I listened to the heartfelt words spoken by many. As the worship leader stood each time to introduce the speakers on the program, I was puzzled, *how do I know this man?* Although I had never seen him before, there was something so familiar about him — his voice. I was so intrigued by the familiarity that my focus shifted from mourning the loss of Keyna to trying to figure out who he was. Each time he stood to introduce a speaker, his voice became a little more familiar. When he began to give the eulogy, I finally recognized his voice, Pastor Gool! It was as if Keyna had introduced him to me at the point I recognized him and saying, "Sonya, this is Pastor Gool." I could even picture her sitting behind him with a bright smile on her face and even remembered her candid laughter. It finally occurred to me to look in the program to confirm whether it was he or not, and after reading through the list, it was confirmed, Pastor Gool of Victory Christian Center in Charlotte, North Carolina. I thought to myself, *oh my gosh! That is how I know him* and I suddenly thought back to the tape Keyna had given me over ten years ago — I could not believe it. At that moment, it was as if she had enthusiastically handed me another CD of one of his sermons.

Although I did not get to attend Pastor Gool's church with Keyna while she was alive — she gave me a unique and special surprise, I was able to hear Pastor Gool preach in person. Even in her death, she caused me to smile and cry all at the same time.

> "And he arose, and rebuked the wind, and said unto the sea, Peace, be still. And the wind ceased, and there was a great calm. And he said unto them, Why are ye so fearful?"
>
> (Mark 4:39 — 40, KJV)